MOUNTAIN LANGUAGE

MOUNTAIN LANGUAGE

HAROLD PINTER

GROVE PRESS
New York

The name Grove Press and the colophon printed on the
title page and outside of this book are trademarks
registered in the U.S. Patent and Trademark Office and in
other countries.

Published by Grove Press
a division of Wheatland Corporation
841 Broadway
New York, N.Y. 10003

Library of Congress Cataloging-in-Publication Data
Pinter, Harold, 1930–
    Mountain language.
    I. Title.
PR6066.I53M65   1989   822′.914   88-35782
ISBN 0-8021-1157-2 (alk. paper)
ISBN 0-8021-3168-9 (pbk. : alk. paper)

Manufactured in the United States of America

This book is printed on acid-free paper.

First Edition 1989

10 9 8 7 6 5 4 3 2 1

To
Antonia

MOUNTAIN LANGUAGE

Mountain Language
was first performed
at the National Theatre
in London on October 20, 1988.

The cast was as follows:

Miranda Richardson

Eileen Atkins

Michael Gambon

Julian Wadham

George Harris

Tony Haygarth

Alex Hardy

Douglas McFerran

Designed by Michael Taylor
Directed by Harold Pinter

CHARACTERS

———————

YOUNG WOMAN

ELDERLY WOMAN

SERGEANT

OFFICER

GUARD

PRISONER

HOODED MAN

SECOND GUARD

I

A PRISON WALL

———————

A line of women. An ELDERLY WOMAN, *cradling her hand. A basket at her feet. A* YOUNG WOMAN *with her arm around the* WOMAN's *shoulders.*

A SERGEANT *enters, followed by an* OFFICER. *The* SERGEANT *points to the* YOUNG WOMAN.

SERGEANT

Name?

YOUNG WOMAN

We've given our names.

SERGEANT

Name?

YOUNG WOMAN

We've given our names.

SERGEANT

Name?

OFFICER (*To* SERGEANT)

Stop this shit. (*To* YOUNG WOMAN) Any
complaints?

YOUNG WOMAN

She's been bitten.

OFFICER

Who?

Pause.

Who? Who's been bitten?

YOUNG WOMAN

She has. She has a torn hand. Look. Her
hand has been bitten. This is blood.

SERGEANT (*To* YOUNG WOMAN)

What is your name?

OFFICER

Shut up.

He walks over to ELDERLY WOMAN.

What's happened to your hand? Has
someone bitten your hand?

The WOMAN *slowly lifts her hand. He peers at it.*

Who did this? Who bit you?

> YOUNG WOMAN
A Doberman pinscher.

> OFFICER
Which one?

Pause.

Which one?

Pause.

Sergeant!

SERGEANT *steps forward.*

> SERGEANT
Sir!

> OFFICER
Look at this woman's hand. I think the thumb is going to come off. (*To* ELDERLY WOMAN) Who did this?

She stares at him.

Who did this?

A big dog.

What was his name?

Pause.

What was his *name*?

Pause.

Every dog has a *name*! They answer to their
name. They are given a name by their
parents and that is their name, that is their
name! Before they bite, they *state* their
name. It's a formal procedure. They state
their name and then they bite. What was
his name? If you tell me one of our dogs bit
this woman without giving his name I will
have that dog shot!

Silence.

Now – attention! Silence and attention!
Sergeant!

SERGEANT
Sir?

17

OFFICER
Take any complaints.

SERGEANT
Any complaints? Has anyone got any
complaints?

YOUNG WOMAN
We were told to be here at nine o'clock this
morning.

SERGEANT
Right. Quite right. Nine o'clock this
morning. Absolutely right. What's your
complaint?

YOUNG WOMAN
We were here at nine o'clock this morning.
It's now five o'clock. We have been standing
here for eight hours. In the snow. Your men
let Doberman pinschers frighten us. One
bit this woman's hand.

OFFICER
What was the name of this dog?

She looks at him.

YOUNG WOMAN
I don't know his name.

SERGEANT

With permission sir?

OFFICER

Go ahead.

SERGEANT

Your husbands, your sons, your fathers,
these men you have been waiting to see, are
shithouses. They are enemies of the State.
They are shithouses.

The OFFICER *steps towards the* WOMEN.

OFFICER

Now hear this. You are mountain people.
You hear me? Your language is dead. It is
forbidden. It is not permitted to speak your
mountain language in this place. You cannot
speak your language to your men. It is not
permitted. Do you understand? You may not
speak it. It is outlawed. You may only speak
the language of the capital. That is the only
language permitted in this place. You will
be badly punished if you attempt to speak
your mountain language in this place. This
is a military decree. It is the law. Your
language is forbidden. It is dead. No one is
allowed to speak your language. Your
language no longer exists. Any questions?

YOUNG WOMAN
I do not speak the mountain language.

Silence. The OFFICER *and* SERGEANT *slowly circle her. The* SERGEANT *puts his hand on her bottom.*

SERGEANT
What language do you speak? What language do you speak with your arse?

OFFICER
These women, Sergeant, have as yet committed no crime. Remember that.

SERGEANT
Sir! But you're not saying they're without sin?

OFFICER
Oh, no. Oh, no, I'm not saying that.

SERGEANT
This one's full of it. She bounces with it.

OFFICER
She doesn't speak the mountain language.

The WOMAN *moves away from the*
SERGEANT'*s hand and turns to face the two*
men.

YOUNG WOMAN
My name is Sara Johnson. I have come to
see my husband. It is my right. Where is he?

OFFICER
Show me your papers.

She gives him a piece of paper. He examines
it, turns to SERGEANT.

He doesn't come from the mountains. He's
in the wrong batch.

SERGEANT
So is she. She looks like a fucking
intellectual to me.

OFFICER
But you said her arse wobbled.

SERGEANT
Intellectual arses wobble the best.

Blackout

2

VISITORS ROOM

———————

A PRISONER *sitting. The* ELDERLY WOMAN
sitting, with basket. A GUARD *standing
behind her.*

The PRISONER *and the* WOMAN *speak in a
strong rural accent.*

Silence.

ELDERLY WOMAN
I have bread —

The GUARD *jabs her with a stick.*

GUARD
Forbidden. Language forbidden.

She looks at him. He jabs her.

It's forbidden. (*To* PRISONER) Tell her to
speak the language of the capital.

PRISONER

She can't speak it.

Silence.

She doesn't speak it.

Silence.

ELDERLY WOMAN

I have apples —

The GUARD *jabs her and shouts.*

GUARD

Forbidden! Forbidden forbidden forbidden!
Jesus Christ! (*To* PRISONER) Does she
understand what I'm saying?

PRISONER

No.

GUARD

Doesn't she?

He bends over her.

Don't you?

She stares up at him.

PRISONER

She's old. She doesn't understand.

GUARD

Whose fault is that?

He laughs.

Not mine, I can tell you. And I'll tell you another thing. I've got a wife and three kids. And you're all a pile of shit.

Silence.

PRISONER

I've got a wife and three kids.

GUARD

You've what?

Silence.

You've got what?

Silence.

What did you say to me? You've got what?

Silence.

You've got *what?*

He picks up the telephone and dials one digit.

Sergeant? I'm in the Blue Room . . . yes . . . I thought I should report, Sergeant . . . I think I've got a joker in here.

Lights to half. The figures are still.

Voices over:

   ELDERLY WOMAN'S VOICE
The baby is waiting for you.

   PRISONER'S VOICE
Your hand has been bitten.

   ELDERLY WOMAN'S VOICE
They are all waiting for you.

   PRISONER'S VOICE
They have bitten my mother's hand.

   ELDERLY WOMAN'S VOICE
When you come home there will be such a welcome for you. Everyone is waiting for you. They're all waiting for you. They're all waiting to see you.

Lights up. The SERGEANT *comes in.*

SERGEANT

What joker?

Blackout

3

VOICE IN THE DARKNESS

SERGEANT'S VOICE
Who's that fucking woman? What's that
fucking woman doing here? Who let that
fucking woman through that fucking door?

SECOND GUARD'S VOICE
She's his wife.

Lights up.

A corridor.

A HOODED MAN *held up by the* GUARD *and
the* SERGEANT. *The* YOUNG WOMAN *at a
distance from them, staring at them.*

SERGEANT
What is this, a reception for Lady Duck Muck?
Where's the bloody Babycham? Who's got
the bloody Babycham for Lady Duck Muck?

He goes to the YOUNG WOMAN.

Hello, Miss. Sorry. A bit of a breakdown in administration, I'm afraid. They've sent you through the wrong door. Unbelievable. Someone'll be done for this. Anyway, in the meantime, what can I do for you, dear lady, as they used to say in the movies?

Lights to half. The figures are still.

Voices over:

MAN'S VOICE
I watch you sleep. And then your eyes open. You look up at me above you and smile.

YOUNG WOMAN'S VOICE
You smile. When my eyes open I see you above me and smile.

MAN'S VOICE
We are out on a lake.

YOUNG WOMAN'S VOICE
It is spring.

MAN'S VOICE
I hold you. I warm you.

YOUNG WOMAN'S VOICE
When my eyes open I see you above me and smile.

Lights up. The HOODED MAN *collapses. The* YOUNG WOMAN *screams.*

                    YOUNG WOMAN
Charley!

The SERGEANT *clicks his fingers. The* GUARD *drags the* MAN *off.*

                    SERGEANT
Yes, you've come in the wrong door. It must be the computer. The computer's got a double hernia. But I'll tell you what – if you want any information on any aspect of life in this place we've got a bloke comes into the office every Tuesday week, except when it rains. He's right on top of his chosen subject. Give him a tinkle one of these days and he'll see you all right. His name is Dokes. Joseph Dokes.

                    YOUNG WOMAN
Can I fuck him? If I fuck him, will everything be all right?

                    SERGEANT
Sure. No problem.

                    YOUNG WOMAN
Thank you.

Blackout

4

VISITORS ROOM

GUARD. ELDERLY WOMAN. PRISONER.

Silence.

The PRISONER *has blood on his face. He sits trembling. The* WOMAN *is still. The* GUARD *is looking out of a window. He turns to look at them both.*

GUARD
Oh, I forgot to tell you. They've changed the rules. She can speak. She can speak in her own language. Until further notice.

PRISONER
She can speak?

GUARD
Yes. Until further notice. New rules.

Pause.

Mother, you can speak.

Pause.

Mother, I'm speaking to you. You see? We can speak. You can speak to me in our own language.

She is still.

You can speak.

Pause.

Mother. Can you hear me? I am speaking to you in our own language.

Pause.

Do you hear me?

Pause.

It's our language.

Pause.

Can't you hear me? Do you hear me?

She does not respond.

Mother?

GUARD
Tell her she can speak in her own language.
New rules. Until further notice.

PRISONER
Mother?

She does not respond. She sits still.

The PRISONER's *trembling grows. He falls
from the chair on to his knees, begins to
gasp and shake violently.*

The SERGEANT *walks into the room and
studies the* PRISONER *shaking on the floor.*

SERGEANT (*To* GUARD)
Look at this. You go out of your way to
give them a helping hand and they fuck it
up.

Blackout